Maria Beasley

and Life Rafts

By Ellen Labrecque

21st Century
Junior Library

Published in the United States of America by
Cherry Lake Publishing
Ann Arbor, Michigan
www.cherrylakepublishing.com

Content Adviser: Amelia Wenk Gotwals, Ph.D., Associate Professor of Science Education, Michigan State University
Reading Adviser: Marla Conn MS, Ed., Literacy specialist, Read-Ability, Inc.

Photo Credits: © Aneese/iStock, cover; © Master Sgt. Kelly Deitloff/ USCG, 4; © Edwin Verin/Shutterstock Images, 6; © John Butterfield/iStock, 8; © Yurij Omelchenko/Shutterstock Images, 10; © Maria E. Beasley (US258191)/United States Patent and Trademark Office, 12; © Thomas Hunter/Library of Congress, 14; © Pavelk/Shutterstock Images, 16; © holbox/ Shutterstock Images, 18; © Master Sgt. Kelly Deitloff/ USCCG, 20

Library of Congress Cataloging-in-Publication Data
Names: Labrecque, Ellen, author.
Title: Maria Beasley and life rafts / by Ellen Labrecque.
Description: Ann Arbor : Cherry Lake Publishing, [2016] | Series: Women innovators | Series: 21st century junior library |
    Includes bibliographical references and index. | Audience: Grades K-3.
Identifiers: LCCN 2016029707| ISBN 9781634721790 (hardcover) | ISBN 9781634722452 (pdf) |
    ISBN 9781634723114 (pbk.) | ISBN 9781634723770 (ebook)
Subjects: LCSH: Beasley, Maria, 1847—Juvenile literature. | Life rafts—History—Juvenile literature. |
    Women inventors—Biography—Juvenile literature. | Inventors—Biography—Juvenile literature.
Classification: LCC VK1471 .L33 2016 | DDC 623.88/8 [B]—dc23
LC record available at https://lccn.loc.gov/2016029707

Cherry Lake Publishing would like to acknowledge the work of The Partnership for 21st Century Skills.
Please visit *www.p21.org* for more information.

Printed in the United States of America
Corporate Graphics

CONTENTS

Life rafts save lives!

A Woman

Have you ever taken a cruise or ridden on a ferry? If so, you may have noticed that these boats carry **life rafts**. If a boat catches fire or begins to sink, life rafts are very important. Passengers can jump on and either row to shore or wait for rescuers.

More than 130 years ago, Maria Beasley **invented** a life raft that was safe and easy to use. Thanks to her invention, countless lives have been saved!

Maria enjoyed helping her father out at their mill.

Maria Kenny was born in the southern United States in 1847. Her father worked as a **miller**. Maria was a curious student. She wanted to learn about everything. Her favorite subjects were math and drawing. When she came home from school, she spent time at her father's **mill**. She drew ideas for ways to improve the milling work!

Create!

Beasley tried to improve machines that were already made. Is there anything you use today that could be improved? Create a detailed drawing of your new invention. Include instructions about how it will work.

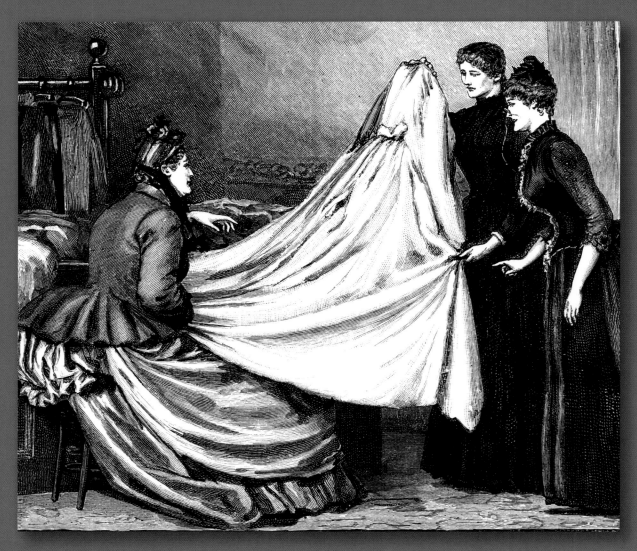

Beasley applied her creativity to making dresses.

In 1865, Maria married Samuel Beasley. She moved to Philadelphia, Pennsylvania. While living there, she worked as a housewife and a dressmaker. Beasley's mind was always filled with new ideas. She wanted to invent many new things.

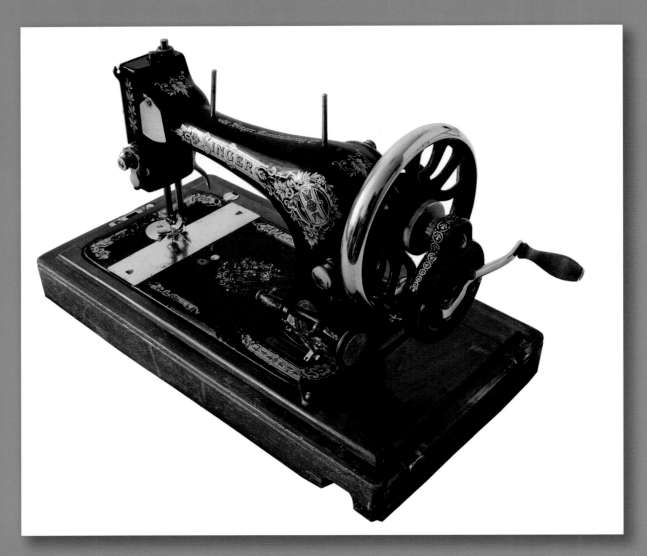

Many of the inventions Beasley saw at the World's Fair
are common today, like the sewing machine!

In 1876, Beasley attended the World's Fair in Philadelphia. Many new inventions were on display, such as typewriters, sewing machines, and the first telephone. The fair inspired Beasley to get to work on her own inventions!

M. E. BEASLEY.

LIFE RAFT.

No. 258,191.   Patented May 16, 1882.

Fig. 1.

Fig. 3.

Fig. 2.

Witnesses: Inventor:
P. C. Dieterich.   M. E. Beasley
Geo. Brinkenburg   per

N. PETERS, Photo-Lithographer, Washington, D. C.

To get her patent, Beasley made detailed
drawings of her invention.

An Idea

One of Beasley's first inventions was a life raft. Beasley kept hearing news about people drowning at sea. She wanted to stop that from happening. On April 6, 1880, she was awarded a **patent** for her life raft. The patent included her description. She wrote that she "invented a certain new and useful Life-Raft, for the purpose of saving life in case of shipwreck."

Before television and the Web, world's fairs were a very important way for inventors to share their ideas with the public.

Beasley's life raft had special features that made it particularly useful. It had **guardrails** to keep people from falling off. It could also be folded in half while being stored. This helped save space on the ships. In 1884, Beasley showed off her life raft at the World's Fair in New Orleans, Louisiana.

Look!

Look at Beasley's raft design on page 12. Describe what you see. Would you want to be rescued on this life raft? Why or why not?

When Beasley was alive, wooden barrels were an important means of transporting food like flour and pickles.

The life raft wasn't Beasley's only invention. She also invented a barrel-making machine, a foot warmer, and a device that kept trains from derailing. Beasley made $20,000 a year from her barrel-making machine. That was a lot of money in those days.

Along with life rafts, boats must carry life preservers
to keep passengers safe.

A Legacy

Based on Beasley's 1880 design, life rafts have continued to improve over the last century. Today, they are stored in containers and **inflate** when opened. Safety laws have been written, too. Boats must have enough life rafts and **life preservers** to save all the people on board.

Today, life rafts are safer and easier to use than ever before.

Maria Beasley's inventions weren't only smart, they were helpful. Her **legacy** is that life at sea is much safer today. Thousands of people have been saved from drowning, thanks to her invention of the life raft!

Ask Questions!

Ask an adult to explain how applying for a patent works. Can a kid invent something and get a patent for it? Try to find more information about patents on the Internet.

GLOSSARY

guardrails (GAHRD-raylz) railing placed along the edge of a boat or highway at dangerous points, as protection

inflate (in-FLAYT) to puff up or fill with air

invented (in-VENT-id) created something new from imagination

legacy (LEG-uh-see) something handed down from one generation to another

life preservers (LIFE pri-ZUR-verz) jackets or belts that keep a person afloat on water

life rafts (LIFE RAFTS) small boats that are used in emergencies

mill (MIL) a building with machines that turn grain into flour

miller (MIL-er) a person who operates a mill

patent (PAT-uhnt) the right granted by the government to use or sell an invention for a certain number of years

FIND OUT MORE

BOOKS

Chin-Lee, Cynthia. *Amelia to Zora: Twenty-six Women Who Changed the World*. Watertown, MA: Charlesbridge, 2008.

McCann, Michelle Roehm. *Girls Who Rocked the World: Heroines from Joan of Arc to Mother Teresa*. New York: Aladdin/Hillsboro, OR: Beyond Words, 2012.

Schatz, Kate. *Rad American Women A-Z*. San Francisco: City Lights Books, 2015.

WEB SITES

Famous Women Inventors
www.women-inventors.com
Learn about other famous women inventors.

National Inventors Hall of Fame
http://invent.org
Check out our country's top inventors.

INDEX

ABOUT THE AUTHOR

Ellen Labrecque is a freelance writer living in Yardley, Pennsylvania. Previously, she was a senior editor at Sports Illustrated Kids. Ellen loves to travel and then learn about new places and people that she can write about in her books.